FANCY COFFINS
TO MAKE YOURSELF

Dale Power

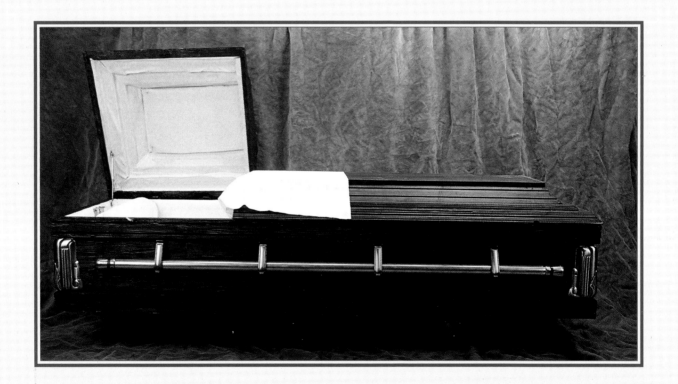

Schiffer Publishing Ltd

4880 Lower Valley Road, Atglen, PA 19310 USA

Copyright © 2001 by Dale L. Power
Library of Congress Card Number: 00-108916

Designed by John P. Cheek
Type set in Zapf Chancery Bd BT/Aldine 721 BT

ISBN: 0-7643-1249-9
Printed in China

Published by Schiffer Publishing Ltd.
4880 Lower Valley Road
Atglen, PA 19310
Phone: (610) 593-1777; Fax: (610) 593-2002
E-mail: Schifferbk@aol.com
Please visit our web site catalog at
www.schifferbooks.com
We are always looking for people to write books on new and related subjects. If you have an idea for a book please contact us at the above address.

This book may be purchased from the publisher.
Include $3.95 for shipping.
Please try your bookstore first.
You may write for a free catalog.

In Europe, Schiffer books are distributed by
Bushwood Books
6 Marksbury Ave.
Kew Gardens
Surrey TW9 4JF England
Phone: 44 (0)20 8 392-8585
Fax: 44 (0)20 8 392-9876
E-mail: Bushwd@aol.com
Free postage in the UK. Europe: air mail at cost

Contents

CAS,
2018 HAPPY
BiRTHDAY!
& HAPPY
WOODWORKING

Jimmy
x

Introduction

For years I have been interested in coffins — their history, construction, and traditions. I hope to give everyone a chance to explore these fascinating objects around which so much history, ceremony, and emotion revolves.

Coffin making has always been a grave matter; throughout time people have used boxes of one sort or another to contain the bodies of their loved ones for their eternal sleep. Coffins have had many names: sarcophagus, casket, coffin, and "the old pine box."

In this book we will explore many of the techniques available to make beautiful, fancy coffins for you and your loved-ones.

Materials and Tools

Plans

Detailed plans for the coffin project have been provided. Be sure to refer to them often while working through the individual construction steps of the coffin.

Wood

The wood used for this project includes cabinet grade plywood with a hardwood veneer and 3/4" hardwood boards to make the molding.

Tools

Woodworking tools required to complete this project include: a planer, safety glasses, a table saw, dado blades to use on the table saw, a jointer, Gorilla Glue, clamps, a screwdriver, a power sander and sand paper of varying grits, a power drill with assorted bits, a hammer and an air hammer, a hand held saw, a route, a router table and assorted bits to make the molding, and satin lining material, 1/2" foam rubber, spray adhesive, double back carpet tape, and a sheet of 1/4" plywood.

Finishes

The exterior finished used in this project is black walnut stain. For the application of stains, wear rubber gloves. You will also find a 1 1/2" synthetic brush useful.

Hardware

Exterior hardware, hinges and locks are available through Rockler Woodworking and Hardware. Call 1-800-279-4441 for a catalog.

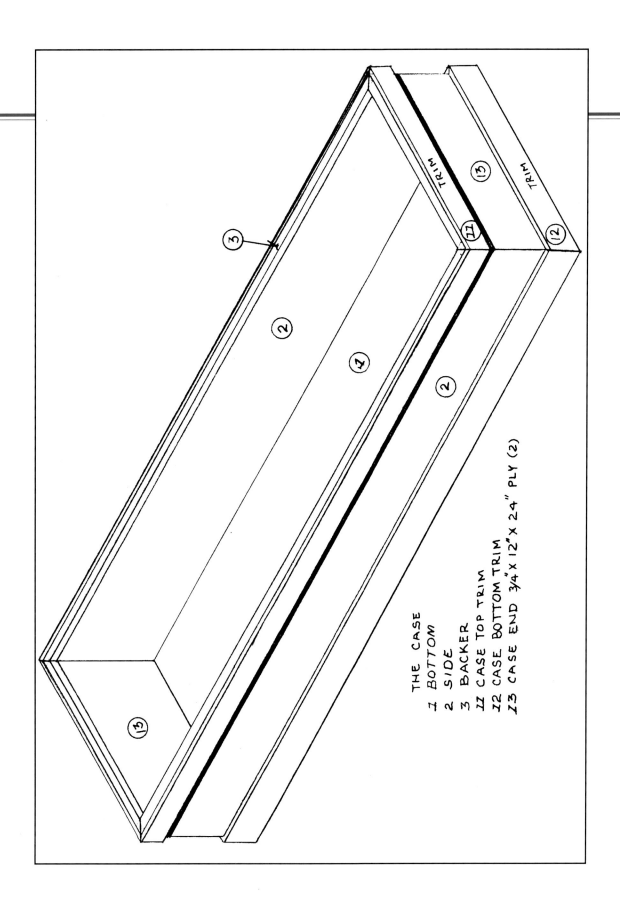

THE CASE
1 BOTTOM
2 SIDE
3 BACKER
11 CASE TOP TRIM
12 CASE BOTTOM TRIM
13 CASE END 3/4" X 12" X 24" PLY (2)

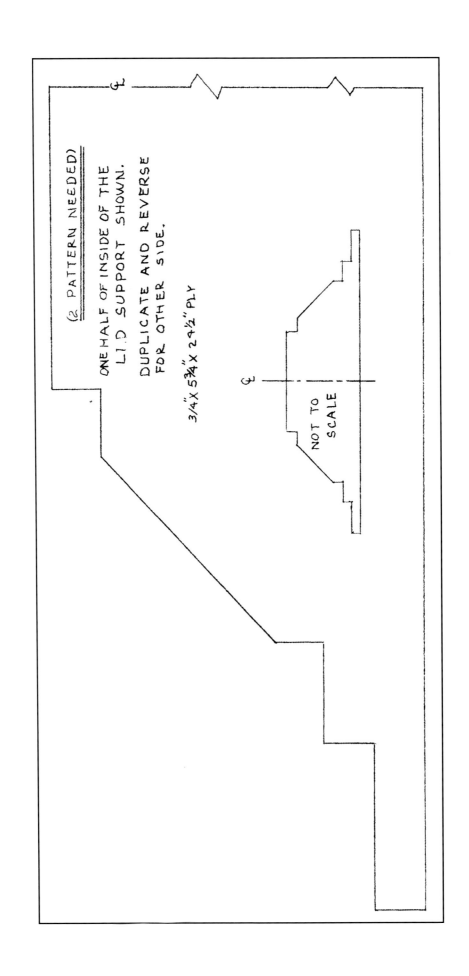

(2 PATTERN NEEDED)

ONE HALF OF INSIDE OF THE
LID SUPPORT SHOWN.

DUPLICATE AND REVERSE
FOR OTHER SIDE.

3/4" X 5¾" X 2½" PLY

NOT TO
SCALE

6

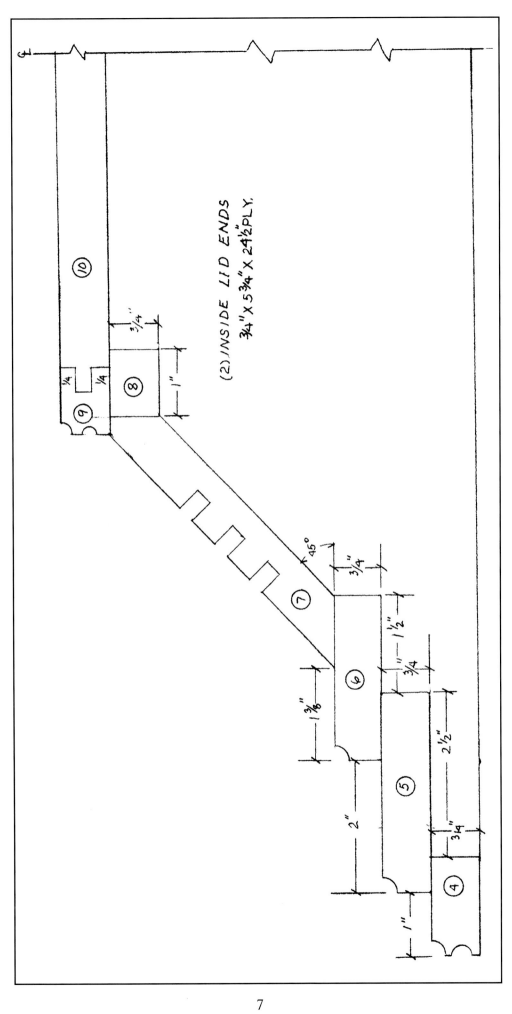

(2) INSIDE LID ENDS
3/4" X 5 3/4" X 24 1/2" PLY.

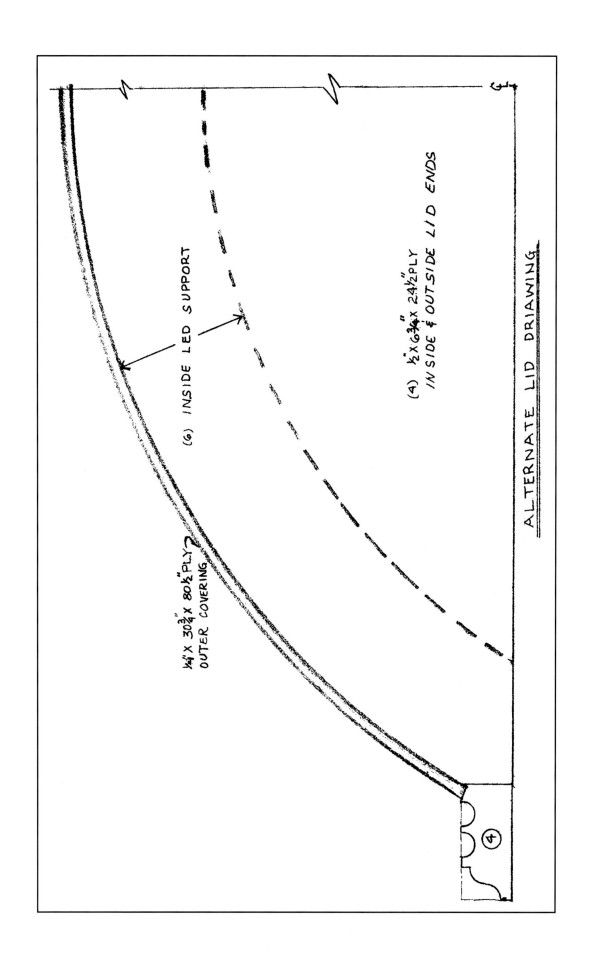

¼" x 30¾" x 80½" PLY
OUTER COVERING

(6) INSIDE LED SUPPORT

½" x 6¾" x 24½" PLY
(4) INSIDE & OUTSIDE LID ENDS

ALTERNATE LID DRIAWING

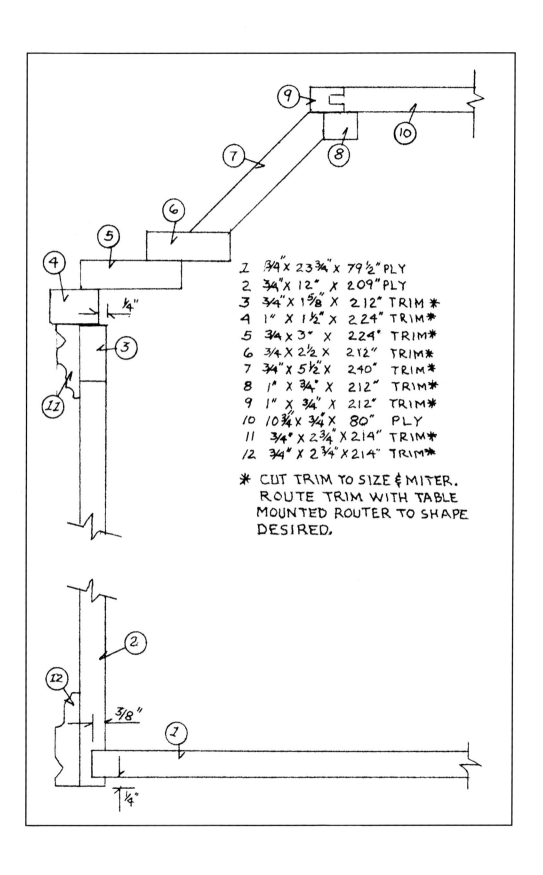

1 3/4" X 23 3/4" x 79 1/2" PLY
2 3/4" X 12" X 209" PLY
3 3/4" X 1 5/8" X 212" TRIM *
4 1" X 1 1/2" X 224" TRIM *
5 3/4 x 3" X 224" TRIM *
6 3/4 X 2 1/2 X 212" TRIM *
7 3/4" X 5 1/2" X 240" TRIM *
8 1" X 3/4" X 212" TRIM *
9 1" X 3/4" X 212" TRIM *
10 10 3/4" X 3/4" X 80" PLY
11 3/4" X 2 3/4" X 214" TRIM *
12 3/4" X 2 3/4" X 214" TRIM *

* CUT TRIM TO SIZE & MITER.
ROUTE TRIM WITH TABLE
MOUNTED ROUTER TO SHAPE
DESIRED.

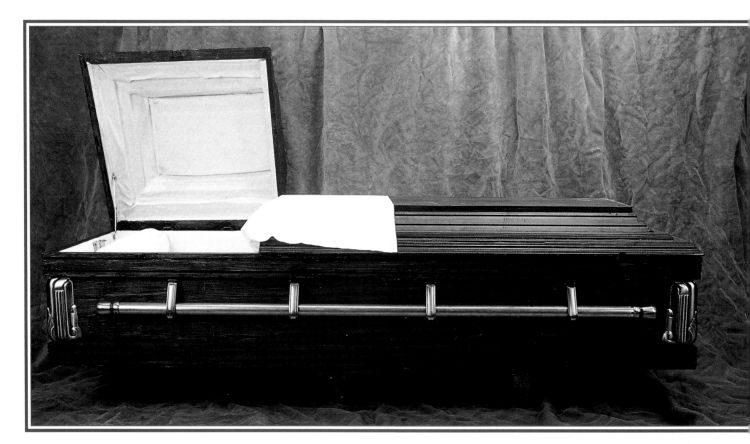

The coffin itself, as it will look when the project is complete.

Constructing the Coffin

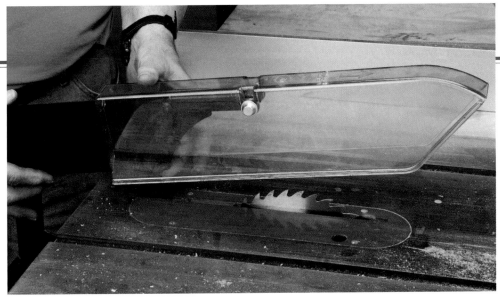

All of the tools and hardware used to create this project may be obtained from your local Rockler Woodworking and Hardware. As always, read the instructions on — and understand all of the safety points of — all of the equipment you use. Always leave the safety guards in place. You will notice that the safety guard on the table saw is being removed. This is for photographic purposes only.

Never trust the measuring tape on your saw. Always use your tape measure, taking your measurements from any of the teeth that are closest to the fence. We are setting the fence at 12" from the blade to cut the height of the side of the coffin.

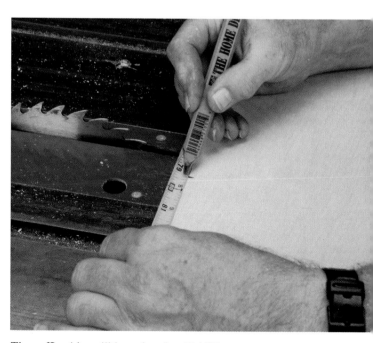

Keep your hands well away from the cutting area as you work.

Rip your plywood to a manageable size. (Normally, ¾" plywood weighs 94 pounds for a 4 x 8 foot sheet. For your final cuts it is nice to have the wood at a manageable size, significantly reducing the weight.) The initial cut brings the sides of the coffin down to 12" wide x 97 ¾" long pieces.

The coffin sides will be reduced to 79 ¾" long.

Rough cut the end boards of the coffin, leaving them several inches oversized (about 26 ½" to 27"). This way, we can do our fine cutting later when the end boards are reduced to a size that is easier to handle.

Use the miter square on the long side of the board to keep it square as you push it through the blade. Never put pressure on both sides of the board during the cut. If you do, the small side of the board may kick back. (Avoid standing directly in front of the blade as well. Standing to one side of the blade will help protect you from an accidental kick back should it occur.) The second sideboard is successfully cut.

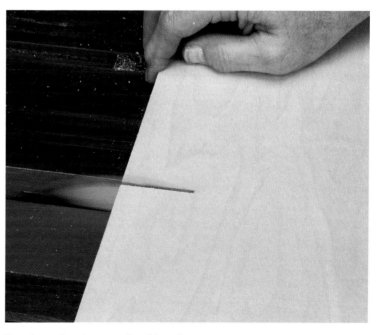

Rough cutting the second end board.

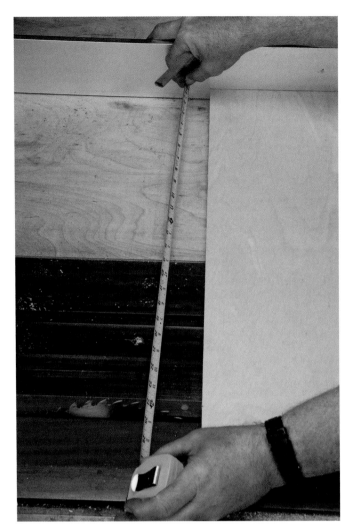

Set the final cut length for the ends of the coffin at 24 1/2" in length.

Keep the wood firmly against the guide as you cut.

Now it is time to install the dado blades on the table saw. It is a good idea to check the size of your plywood before you put the dado head in place. Plywood is not sized exactly. This plywood, although called ¾" thick, is actually slightly less.

Line up the chipper so that it does not match up with the teeth on the outside blade.

In this case, it takes two outside blades and four chippers to match the thickness of this ¾" plywood.

All of the chippers are in place. The chipper blades are staggered as well.

Line up the last space in the last blade with the tooth of the last chipper blade as shown.

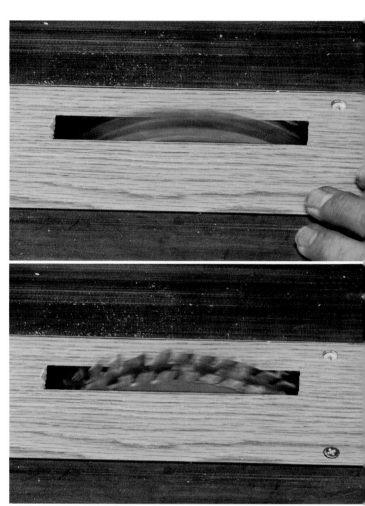

Raise the blade up with the saw running to check your clearance. The blade should not bind or catch on the plate while you are running the saw.

Lower your blade below the surface of the plate.

Set the dado to a height of 3/8".

Set the clearance from the fence at ¼". This dado is being cut to hold the bottom of the coffin in place.

The dado cuts are in place on the lower edge of the side and end boards of the coffin to hold the base in place.

Above & top right: Run a sample board through the dado to make sure your measurements are exact. The fit is perfect.

Here we have installed a 45-degree locking miter bit in the router table and we are running the cuts for the sides of the casket. The inside of the boards are down.

Running the ends of the casket. The inside of the coffin ends are placed against the fence to put the appropriate miter cut along the inside edge.

The finished cuts allow the joined side and end pieces to lock together.

Now it is time to start assembling to coffin. Gorilla Glue, which is water activated, will be used in the assembly. By putting glue on one side of the joint and water on the other, the water will activate the glue and ensure a tight fit. While the glue is curing we will hold the joints together with 1 1/8" nails driven home from the air nailer.

Trim the bottom to fit the inside dimensions of the coffin, including the dado cut in the side and end pieces.

Applying glue to the joint.

Right: Once both ends are securely attached to the coffin's side panel, use Gorilla Glue along the dado cuts and slide the bottom into place. This will help square up the coffin.

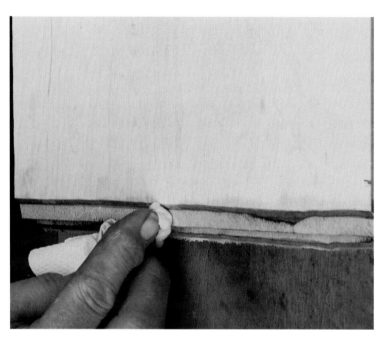

Moistening the other side of the joint with water.

Above & below: Use nails to secure the bottom to the sides for a tight seal while the glue dries. Apply glue to the exposed edges of the sides and bottom of the coffin.

Make sure your joints are square and nail the joint tightly together. One end is now attached to one side of the coffin.

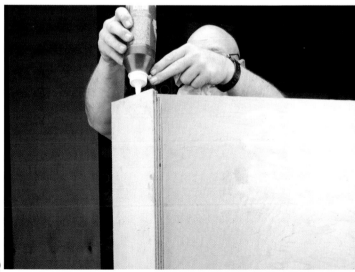

Slip the other side in place and make sure it fits well. Set this assembled coffin base aside to dry.

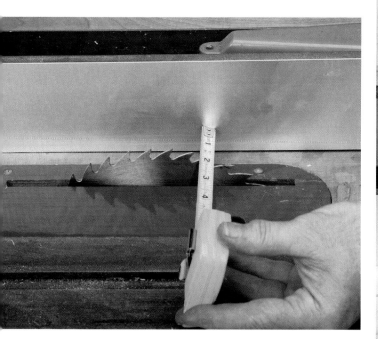

We will now begin to make the edge trim. Set the saw fence for 1 5/8" wide for cutting the boards that will wrap the top of the coffin. I am using ¾" birch planks to create the wrap.

Cut the birch wrap. As you get to the end of the board, use a pusher stick to help keep your fingers well clear of the blade. Depending on the length of your birch boards, you may have to cut several lengths of 1 5/8" wrap.

Even a fairly narrow birch board
may be trimmed for wrap.

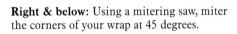

Right & below: Using a mitering saw, miter
the corners of your wrap at 45 degrees.

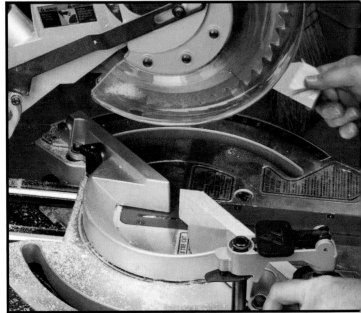

Apply a fine line of Gorilla Glue along the edges of the box.

Moisten the edges of the wrap that will come into contact with the Gorilla Glue.

Put the wrap in place and proceed around the coffin. Remember to apply glue and water to the mitered edges of the wrap as well.

Cut the trim pieces to match the edges of your coffin. Dry fit all the wrap to make sure you have a nice tight fit in all of the corners.

Place several nails in at angles along the length of the wrap as well.

Secure the ends with 1 1/8" nails. Angle one nail through the wrap into the coffin wall along the ends to keep the wrap secure.

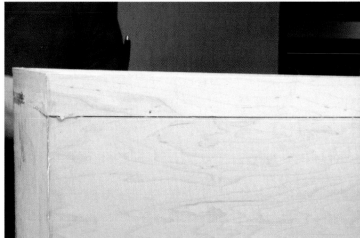

The wrap is in place and secured around the upper edge of the coffin. With the nails in place, set aside the coffin base to dry. While the base dries, we will turn our attentions to making molding for the lid.

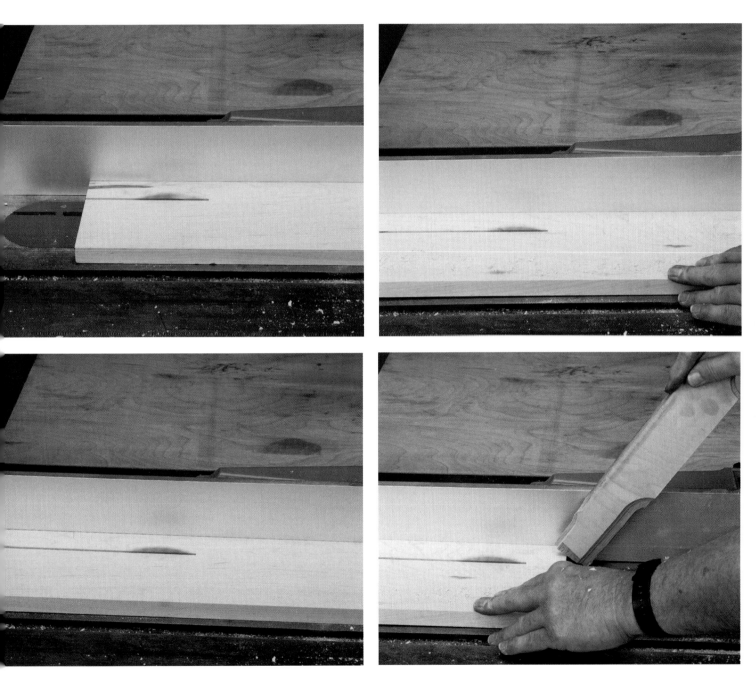

We are going to start cutting the molding. Make sure you have wood of ample length for the size of your coffin. The molding measures 1 ½" wide x 1" thick. Cut all the molding lengths now to save yourself time later. Don' t forget to use your pusher board as you near the end of the board to keep your fingers clear of the blade.

Reset the fence to cut molding pieces measuring 5 ¼" wide x 1" thick.

Cutting 3" x ¾" molding.

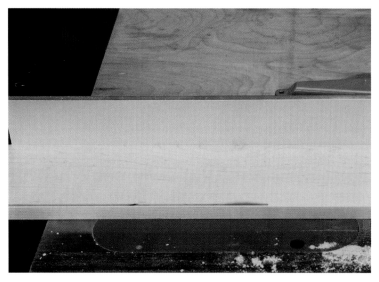

Cutting the molding.

Cutting 2 1/2" x ¾" molding. Remember to cut an appropriate amount for your lid.

Cut a 1" x ¾" backer block to the length you need.

Once they have been cut, run all of the molding edges through a jointer to make them square.

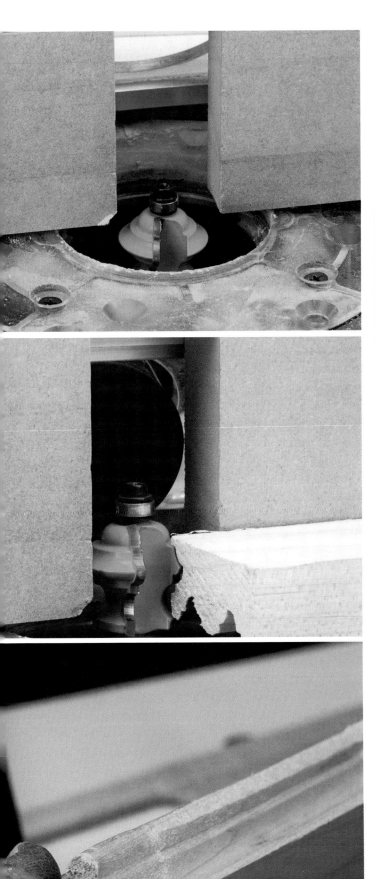

When the wood is turned on edge, this distinctive profile is created, which is a completely different look. With multiple passes through the bit, you can create very complex profiles.

This is a multi-profile router bit. With the bit at its full extension and the wood is on its side, you create a routed profile that looks like this.

This board has taken two passes through the router to create this pattern.

on the second, the molding is standing on edge. This creates an ornate multi-level cut.

For the rest of the molding, we will be making two passes through the router. The first pass has the molding laying down flat on the router table and ...

Pushers of this type make it both easier and safer to run wood through the router.

The multi-level cut is complete on the molding edge.

As you are routing out the molding, check the direction of the grain. If the grain is heading the wrong direction when you cut, you will get tear outs like this.

Continue routing, first with the board lying flat, and then with the board on edge to complete the cut.

Continue routing along the edge of the molding. As you continue, it is a good idea to keep track of which direction the wood was passed through the router last to ensure you end up with molding featuring the proper edge cut.

The second cut of 45 degrees finishes the first molding strip. Note, of course, that this cut is set at the opposite angle to the first cut.

This is the first cut on the molding using a chop saw. Make sure to cut your molding ½" larger than the bottom of the coffin as the lid will extend beyond the base ¼" all the way around. Always remember to let the chop saw blade stop before lifting it away from the wood. Check the cross section drawing of the bottom and top of the coffin as needed.

Continue cutting the molding for the bottom tier of the coffin lid.

Both end pieces for the bottom tier of the lid are now cut.

Care has to be taken when measuring the ends to allow for the ¼" offset from the inside of the box. The first end piece of molding for the bottom tier of the lid is now cut.

Left & below: Glue together the first level of the lid with your Gorilla glue. Nail the joints together as well.

This is a good time to clean up any glue that has risen out of the joints. This may be cleaned away with either a knife or a scraper.

We have now installed the two outside blades of the dado to create the pattern in the moldings.

The blade height is set at 3/8".

While the glued first tier of the coffin lid dries, cut the molding to wrap the upper and lower edges of the coffin with the table saw. I am cutting my molding to a width of 2 ¾". Your width may vary depending on the hardware and the height of the side of your custom coffin. Don't forget to use a scrap of wood as a pusher stick for safety's sake as you reach the end of the board.

Set the table saw fence to 1/2".

Run the molding through the saw.

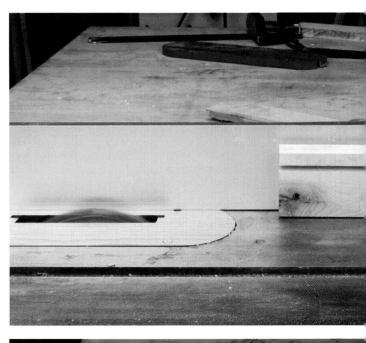

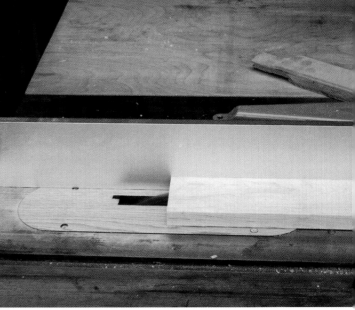

Turn the board around and cut the same groove along the opposite edge of the board.

The first molding cut is in place.

Like so.

Mitering the opposite end to the correct length.

Use the chop saw to miter the molding ends to 45 degrees. Measure the outside perimeter of your coffin and add twice the thickness of your molding to get the correct length to wrap your piece.

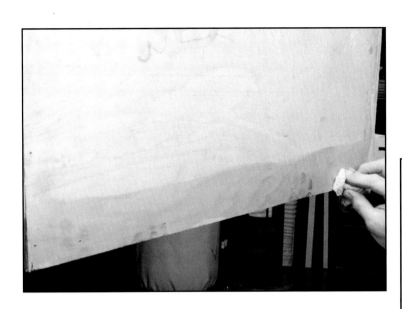

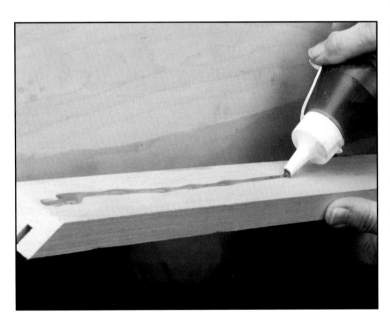

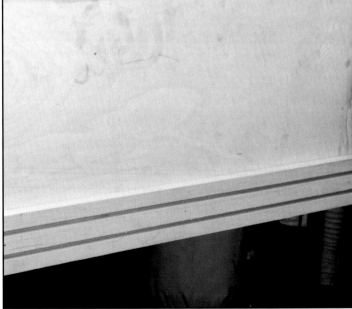

To fasten the molding along the bottom edge of the coffin, dampen the bottom of the coffin with water where the molding will be applied. Apply a line of Gorilla Glue to the inside of the molding and along the angled corner where the glue will come into contact with the next piece of molding. Carefully align the molding with the bottom edge of the coffin. Nail the molding in place. Note that since Gorilla glue expands as it sets, there is no need to apply more than a single line along the back of the molding.

The bottom molding is now in place.

To ensure a proper fit, use a clamp to hold the molding in place along the upper edge of the coffin body and dry fit the molding before gluing it together. Apply the upper molding in the same manner as the lower molding.

Apply water to the coffin and glue to the molding. Roughly three of the 1 1/8" nails will secure the molding while the glue dries. Continue applying molding around the body of the coffin.

To avoid errors such as *this* (where the decorative cuts in the molding are at different distances from the outer edges of the adjacent molding strips), cut all of the molding decoration at the *same time*.

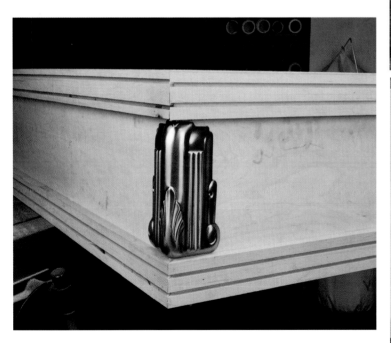

When the molding is in place, dry fit the decorative metal hardware to make sure the fit is proper.

Now we can return to cutting and assembling the lid. There are several possible decorative cuts you could add to complete this decorative lid molding. We will use the dado head to cut two strips 1 ¾" from either side.

Repeat this process until you have enough molding for the second tier of the lid.

The first cut is in place. Turn the board end over end and make the second cut.

Both decorative cuts are now in place.

To make the larger piece of molding we first trim the two edges to 45 degrees. Then we square off the upper edge, creating a platform upon which to fasten the molding for the rest of the lid. To begin, use a single blade on the table saw and tilt that blade to 45 degrees.

Cut the molding at a 45-degree angle with the decorative face down.

The first cut is made.

Continue cutting until all of the molding has been cut at a 45-degree angle along one edge.

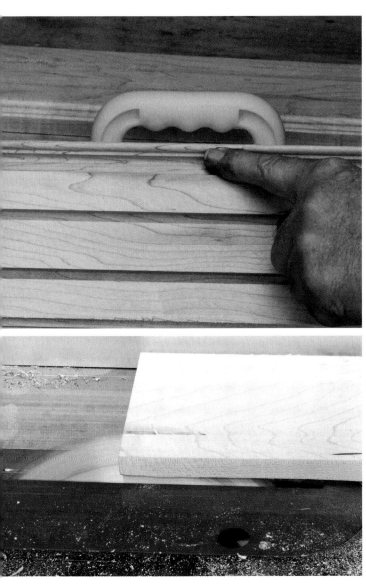

Reverse the molding and move the fence in 5/8" to match the cut on the opposite edge (shown here). Begin cutting.

Now a second cut angled at 45 degrees is made in the opposite direction to the first.

Both ends of the molding are now cut at matching 45 degree angles.

Turn the molding face up. Make that second angled cut along the upper edge to remove enough wood so that the molding that sits above it will have a level platform to rest upon.

The cut has been made. Now the molding will sit square and hold the next tier of molding above it level.

Building a simple jig from scrap wood will help hold your angled molding in place as you cut it with the compound miter saw. You will note from the next photographs that the upper lip of the jig needs to be cut back enough to provide the proper clearance for the saw itself while cutting.

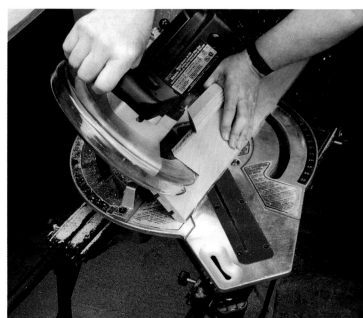

Cutting the angled molding for the lid. This 45-degree angle creates the proper slope for the lid's profile.

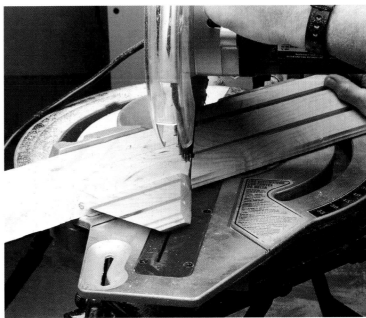

Cutting the molding.

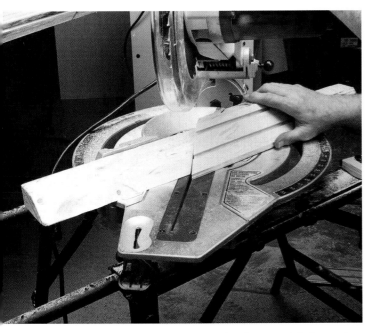

With a compound miter saw, this process has been straightforward. Without it, I would suggest that if you have a miter saw, you take a 2 x 4 on your table saw, rip it at 45 degrees and set it to hold your cove molding at the proper angle. Then go ahead and miter it as you normally would.

Left & below: To begin building the coffin lid from the molding, start with the 3" flat molding. Make your 45 degree angled cuts to fit the pieces together around the lid. Use Gorilla Glue and nails to hold the three inch molding in place and begin to build up the lid.

Continue gluing and nailing molding in place to create the lid. This tier is inset ½" from the inner edge of the tier below. The molding measures 2 ½" wide.

The next layer of molding is now in place.

It is time to place the cove molding. Use your wooden brace to support the cove molding as you cut the proper 45 degree angle, allowing the surface to be angled and yet meet the next piece of cove molding along the side or end. Continue cutting the cove molding at the proper angle.

Left & below: The cove molding is now in place.

Once the cove molding is in place, use a 1" x ¾" wooden wrap along the upper edge of the cove. Make a centered dado cut in the wrap to make a breadboard edge for the plywood top covering the lid. The dado cut is 3/8" deep x ½" high.

Cut the wrap on the compound mitre saw to length, making the necessary 45 degree angle cuts as you go.

This is a 1/8" thick x 3/8" deep rabbeted edge on the plywood top, allowing the breadboard edge of the wrap to fit over the plywood.

Once the breadboard edge is attached to the plywood lid, glue and nail the lid in place. The entire coffin lid is now completely assembled. It is ready to be cut into two sections (one considerably shorter than the other for proper viewing), hinged, and attached to the body of the coffin.

Use glue and nails to secure the wrap to the lid. As movement may occur within the plywood (due to swelling and contraction), you can only nail into the ends of the breadboard. Glue the corners together. You may, however, also place several nails down the sides of the breadboard.

Transfer the pattern from the foam template to your plywood. Cut out both supports on your band saw.

The inside supports for both the long and short sections of the lid are made out of ¾" plywood and cut to fit the interior countours of your coffin lid. You will need two of these supports. Styrofoam makes an excellent template for transferring the pattern from the inside of the lid to your plywood. If you have a band saw, that is the best tool to use to cut out these supports. If not, find a friend who has one!

The glue is dry, the braces are securely in place. Now comes the moment of truth! How well do you cut wood? Use a saber saw to cut between the two braces.

Make sure both braces are properly aligned prior to gluing them in place. Both braces are now glued in place. They should be roughly 4' 6" from the bottom end of the lid and have a 1/8" gap between the two braces. The gap allows room for a wood veneer to be applied in an upcoming step. Set the braced lid aside to dry. These braces will support both sides of the lid once it is cut in two.

You can only cut so far with the lid turned upside down. Turn the lid over to continue making your cut.

Before you proceed, mark in guidelines to follow as the supports are no longer visible to follow with the lid right side up.

Continue carefully cutting to separate the lid completely.

The lid is separated.

Any imperfections caused by the saw may now be removed from the divided halves of the lid and bracing with a rasp. Removing the imperfections also prepares the area for a veneer plate.

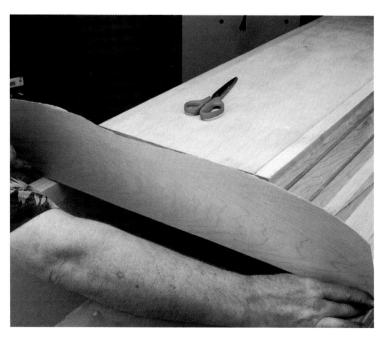

Cut the laminate veneer large enough to extend beyond all of the edges of the lid. A self adhering veneer works as well as any. To ensure that the veneer sticks to the wood: 1) make sure there is no sawdust on the wood; and 2) use a small roller to help flatten the veneer smoothly against the surface of the brace.

Working from the center out, use the roller to adhere the veneer to the brace.

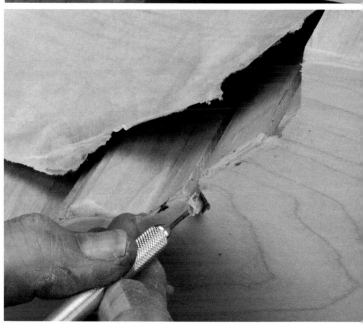

A sander may be used on larger areas (straight surfaces, etc.) to quickly remove excess veneer. An Exacto knife works well for trimming veneer away from the smaller details.

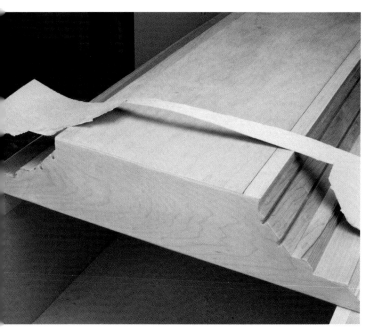

The veneer is in place.

These are special coffin hinges you may purchase from a variety of sources (including Rockler). This is a two-part hinge. Once the hinges are properly secured, the lid may be removed and put back on easily.

Both inside surfaces of the lid are now covered with veneer.

Evenly space the hinges, and mount the top component of the hinge in place on the lid with the screws supplied. A drill driver is very helpful here.

If you are so inclined and equipped, you could remove the necessary wood with a router. I am using a chisel in this instance, however. I suggest that you trim down to your cut first before you try to level out the main body of your work. This will help prevent chip out.

The hinge bases, however, must be countersunk into the coffin body to make sure the lid will close flush with the body. Make sure the bottom and top components of the hinges line up properly before you countersink the hinge bases. Here is one of many methods for countersinking hinges. First mark the area around the outside of the hinge and score that outline with a knife.

Make the surface as level as you can. The hinge base should be flush with the surface of the wood when you are done.

Once each hinge is properly adjusted, a third screw, acting as a locking screw, is put in place.

Components of a coffin lid catch.

Install a separate support hinge as well. This enables the lid to be locked in an upright position. Six screws and a screwdriver are all that are required to install this simple hinge.

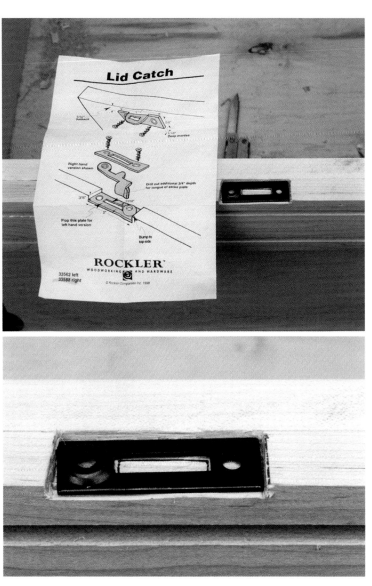

Mortice the locking device into place. You must cut your mortice deep enough to accept two flat metal plates with a locking arm placed between them.

Drill out the center of the lock recess ¾" deep to accept the tongue of the upper catch plate. Mark your drill with a piece of tape at the proper depth.

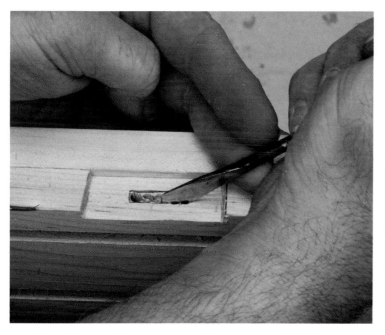

Use a chisel to chip out excess wood between your drill holes.

The lower components of the lid catch are assembled.

The upper component of the lid catch is in place on the lid and properly aligned. The catch is now complete.

When the lid catch is installed, it is almost invisible when locked.

Finishes and Linings for the Coffin

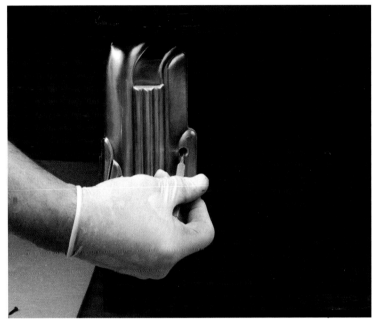

Now that we have all of the hinges attached to the lid, we'll move on to the exterior finishes and interior lining. We are using a combined "gel stain and sealer in one" to stain the coffin in Walnut. Brush the stain on and let it dry. You can wipe off the areas to lighten the color or brush on another coat to darken the coffin.

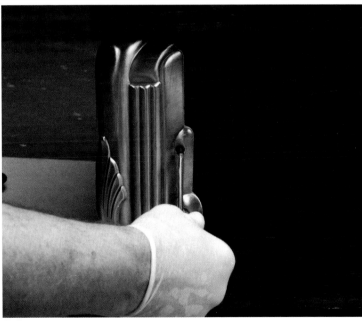

Now it is time to apply the corner hardware. The hardware may be purchased from Rockler Woodworking. This hardware comes with its own screws and is very simple to apply. First use an awl to make guide holes for your screws. Fasten the hardware to the coffin with the screws supplied.

The first coat of stain is applied.

The hardware is in place.

On this coffin, the brackets are being set 16" in from either end and 16" further in for the two interior brackets along the long sides of the coffin. This gives you plenty of lifting support. Place handles on the short ends as well.

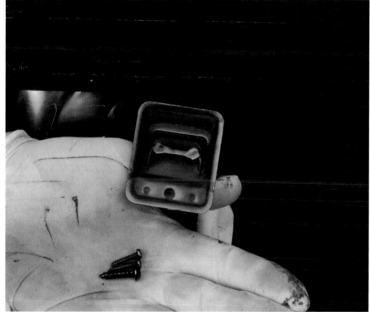

The handle brackets come with three screws each. There are three screws for each bracket: two small screw and one large. All three screws are required to make sure the bracket is secure when the handle is being used.

These end caps are made for either 1 ½" wooden dowels or brass tubing. To secure the handle material to the handle brackets, there are holes in the backs of the brackets for screws. Slide the end caps in place and secure them with screws.

The handles and end caps are now in place.

For an additional finishing touch to your coffin, you may also add ornate decorative details such as this to the exterior. These details are produced in plaster and are easy to attach with glue and stain. These details may also be purchased from Rockler, or from any national woodworking catalog.

Adding a small notch above the lid catch makes it easier to move and engage the catch.

Starting with the coffin body ends, cut plywood backers to start lining the coffin's interior. Adhere one inch thick foam rubber to the ¼" plywood backing with a spray adhesive. Remember to deduct the thickness of the plywood and the foam rubber from the overall length of your interior side backer pieces or they will not fit within the available space.

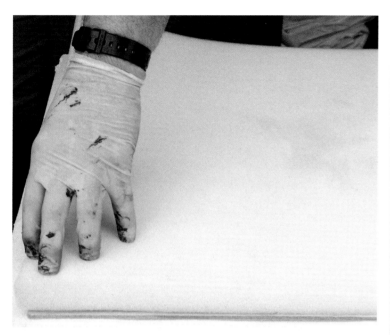

Applying the foam rubber.

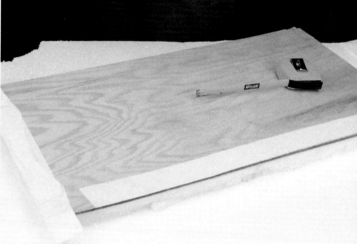

Use double backed tape to secure the fabric in place.

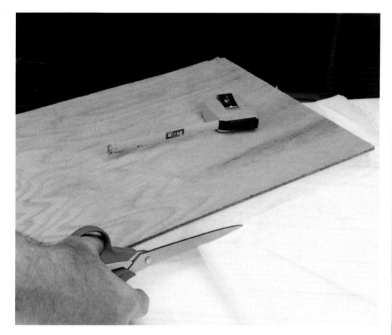

Leave approximately 2" of fabric past the edge of the backer board.

Miter the corners of the fabric so the ends will fold over neatly. Secure the cloth with the tape.

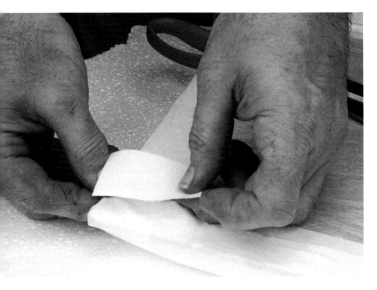

A little double back tape may also be used to hold the corners down.

Your first piece is now ready to go into the coffin.

Secure the cloth and foam covered backer boards in place within the coffin with double back tape. Repeat this process until the interior sides are completely covered. The technique remains the same throughout.

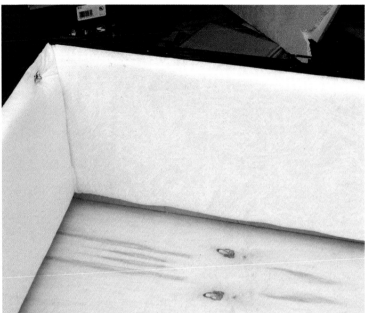

The interior sides are now well covered. Note that the upper lid's support hinge was removed and reinstalled once the upper end backer board was in place.

Line the interior of the lid in the same manner.

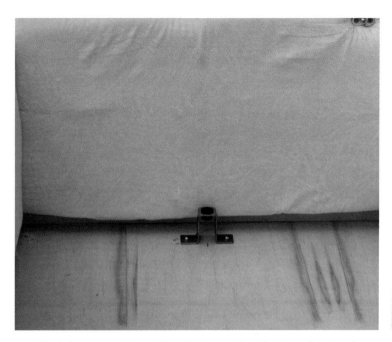

Find the center of the coffin. Make sure that the base of the hardware supporting the casket bed frame is level when you install it along the centerline of the coffin.

The vertical hardware that both supports the bed frame and raises or lowers it is now in place at either end of the coffin. The vertical hardware simply clips into the upper bracket and inserts into the lower bracket.

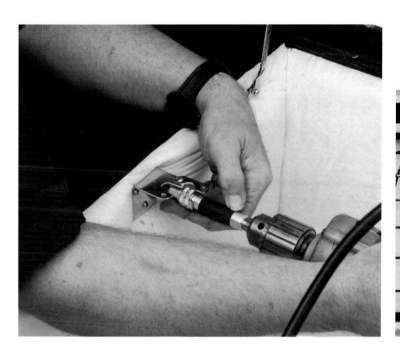

Install the hardware that both supports the frame and raises or lowers either the head or feet. Similar hardware is installed at both ends. The hardware will be hidden from sight by a pillow during viewing. Make sure the bracket at the top is level before installing it.

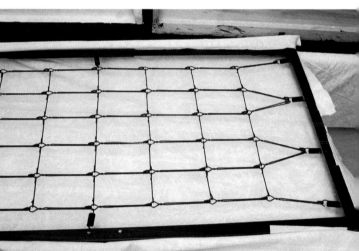

This is the coffin's bed frame.

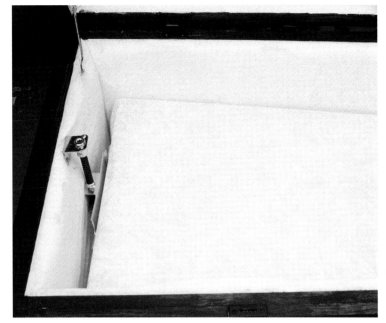

Cover the frame with 1" thick foam and cover the foam with fabric. Insert the bed into the coffin. Attach the vertical hardware to the frame prior to inserting the bed into the coffin. The vertical hardware should socket into the brackets fairly easily.

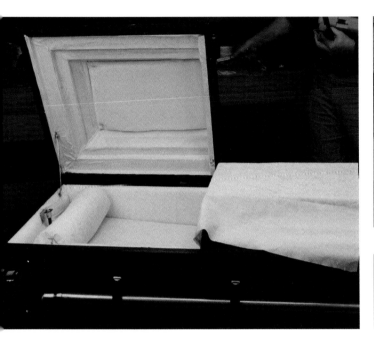

A simple foam pillow covered in the interior fabric and a cloth to cover the opening to the lower half of the coffin finish the project.

The project is complete.

Gallery

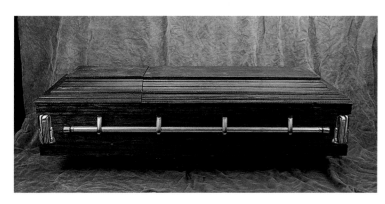

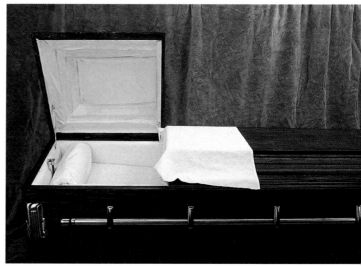

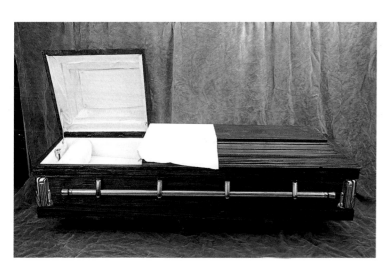

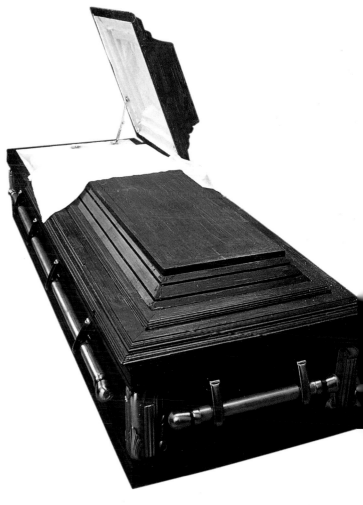